mommy mixology

mommy mixology

A Cocktail for Every Calamity

JANET FRONGILLO

Ulysses Press

Published by:
Ulysses Press
P.O. Box 3440
Berkeley, CA 94703
www.ulyssespress.com

A Hollan Publishing, Inc. Concept

ISBN: 978-1-61243-069-0
Library of Congress Catalog Number 2012937118

Printed in China by Everbest through Four Colour Print Group

10 9 8 7 6 5 4 3 2 1

Acquisitions Editor: Keith Riegert
Managing Editor: Claire Chun
Editor: Rebecca Pepper
Proofreader: Lauren Harrison
Cover design: what!design @ whatweb.com
Cover photos: © judiswinksphotography.com
Author photo on page 112 © Debbie Ellis Photography
Recipes pictured on pages 14, 17, 24, 30, 34, 38, 46, 51, 59, 62, 66, 71, 75, 79, 83, 87, 92, 96, 100, 104 © judiswinksphotography.com
Other interior photos: see page 111
Food stylist for pictured recipes: Anna Hartman-Kenzler

Distributed by Publishers Group West

For Rick, for always believing I could.
And for JP, Tommy, and Will, you are laughter, unbridled
enthusiasm, and love—you are, and always will be, my best work.

Contents

Introduction

Welcome to my corner of the world. I'm so thrilled to have you here—I really hope you stay a while. I'll hold on while you get comfy. (It's only fair. I'm in my snowman jammies. It hurts to be this glamorous. It really does.)

Ready? Then let's get this party started!

So about this book, *Mommy Mixology*. It's the culmination of the many calamities I've experienced while pregnant and mommying over the past seven years. Even my path to becoming a mom was a calamity of sorts. The hubs and I had been married almost five years when our oldest came along. I'd love to say we postponed having kids because I was out saving the world, but really, I was just watching *Big Brother* and other bad reality TV and having some fertility issues. After suffering several miscarriages and the roller coaster of emotions that came with them, we were fortunate enough to inexplicably have three boys in roughly four years. (I have no idea why, and neither does my board-certified, kick-ass doctor. I'm thinking we beat Vegas odds on that one! I really should go buy a lottery ticket.)

Naturally, after the rocky road to parenthood, we were walking on clouds when our oldest was born. (Well, hubs was. I was more shuffling along enjoying the Percocets … but we'll talk about that later. Don't be scared!)

Where are you going? Come back! It's not that bad—after all, I did go on to do it two more times.

I've learned a lot over the past seven years. I've made more mistakes than I care to admit. I'm not an expert. I don't have a degree in child psychology. I'm not a pediatrician. (You're welcome, American Academy of Pediatrics. You're welcome.) I have no cool titles after my name. I don't even work at Babies "R" Us. All I know is that a child, whether biological or adopted, makes you a parent. When it's go time, you do the best you can, and hopefully you never forget what a gift he or she is.

Regardless of whether you plan to stay home with the kids or pick up for a second and third (!) shift at home after busting your butt all day for the man, there will be calamities. And for those, there should be cocktails. *Mommy Mixology* is filled with calamities I've faced, my friends have faced, and, I'm pretty sure, you'll face in the next five years. Each calamity comes with a yummy drink recipe.

I don't have all the answers, but I promise: I'm telling you what I know, straight up. The good, the bad, the ugly, but most of all, the funny. Because honestly? The good, the bad, and the ugly … are mostly pretty damn funny. You'll be barraged with messages, both overt and subtle, from TV shows, catalogs, and movies, images of perfect moms in their perfect clothes in their perfect homes with their perfect kids. Like washboard abs, I'm convinced, no such thing exists. I'm calling bullshit on all of that right now. (Maybe not on the washboard abs. Not everyone has doughy Irish DNA.)

So when your pants won't button, and your baby spits up all over you in your last clean shirt because you're behind on laundry, and your family room looks like a stage-5 hurricane ripped through, and you realize you can't make dinner because all you have in the house is Enfamil and Cheerios, and, and, and … breathe! Do not panic. I totally get it. Most moms, if they're being honest, get it.

When you feel like the worst mother in the world because your toddler gets hurt on your watch and winds up in the ER, I get it.

When your three-year-old swears in the deli line, and everyone turns and stares and you feel like Hester Prynne, 21st century? Been there.

When you feel like you're going to hurl after your kindergartner's bus pulls away on the first day of school, I know … you need a hug.

This gig ain't easy. But it's so worth it. And there's no need to be a martyr! You don't have to vacuum in pearls, your house doesn't have to be a museum, and stuff won't always get done when you want. In five days, or five months, or five years, it won't matter. What will matter is that you loved your child and he knew it. It's not that complicated.

So how about that drink now? Emergentini? Scarlet A? Cosmopotty? Take a sip, read, and feel free to learn from my mistakes. Just do me one favor:

Have your cocktail at home or make friends with a teetotaler! Drinking and driving is unbecoming for a mommy. (And for all I know, you only weigh like 105 pounds. I still like you, though. I do!) I know you wouldn't want to hurt someone else's mama or baby on the road.

Seriously. Some of your best days are here. Right here, right now. Cheers, mama—something tells me you're going to be more than great.

CHAPTER ONE

Conception

You're pregnant? Congratulations. You did it! (At least once—that I know of. Go you!) Really, that extra line on the stick is truly life changing. Now: all those scary stories you've heard about pregnancy and labor? Forget 'em. Just listen to mine instead. (I'm kidding ~~a little~~.) I recommend you use your pregnancy to tinkle alone and rest up—since you won't get to do either again until the cherub hits the tween years and wants nothing to do with you. Also, and I'm so seriously serious about this, don't even think about signing on for the parenting gig if you don't have a sense of humor. What's the point if you can't see the funny? There's a fine line between laughing and crying sometimes, and besides, ~~mostly~~ everything is repairable. (But now would be a good time to unload that white couch on Craigslist!)

Fertile Myrtle Mimosa

Whether you've been trying for years or it was literally, um, a stab in the dark, when you announce your big news, everyone wants to celebrate. In a world where bad news seems to reign supreme, everyone loves a pregnant lady. So sing it, sister. Tell everyone you know—friends, family, the butcher, the baker, the candlestick maker, everyone!

Just remember, it's not 1972. We wear seat belts now, take vitamins, and bathe in sunblock. You know you can't get your drink on for the next nine (wait—is now a bad time to tell you it's really more like ten?) months. No problem, hot mama. Toast your fab news with a Fertile Myrtle Mimosa.

makes 1 serving

⅓ cup chilled sparkling cider
⅓ cup chilled orange juice
Fresh lemon juice

Add the sparkling cider to a champagne flute, then pour in the orange juice. Stir. Squeeze in lemon juice to taste.

Watermelon Weigh-In

When I was preggers and feeling every bit like a swollen watermelon, I was indignant that they weighed me right in the hallway. "Who the hell planned that?" I screamed inside my hormonal head. In an office full of women with not a man in sight to blame, I wanted names.

But I had to laugh when the hubs looked like he wanted to evaporate into the wall when I'd get weighed. I mean, the dude has seen me naked. When someone's seen you naked, isn't the number sorta meaningless? I finally just told him straight up, "Hey, no need to lurk by the wallpaper like you're not the baby daddy. You did this to me, remember?" (The sooner husbands accept blame for practically everything, the better.)

So just go with it—enjoy this time when calories and numbers don't count. (Unless your doctor specifically says, "Put the fork down, woman!" which did happen to one of my friends.)

makes 1 serving

¾ cup watermelon chunks

1 tablespoon fresh lime juice

2 teaspoons sugar

Dash of salt

Handful of ice cubes

Watermelon slice, for garnish (optional)

Lime wedges, for garnish (optional)

Place the watermelon, lime juice, sugar, salt, and ice in a blender and blend to the desired consistency. Pour into a glass. Garnish with sliced watermelon and a lime wedge, if desired.

Paddy O'Preggo

If you're lucky, you'll glide through pregnancy glowing. My first pregnancy was like that. I felt great, didn't gain much weight, and was all smug with myself. (I know. I want to punch me in the face, too.) The second and third pregnancies? I think it's called comeuppance? Yeah, that.

Do you have a headache so wretched you'd swear a thousand tiny garden gnomes were chiseling away at your brain, while you struggle to keep down Saltines? Do you wake up in the fetal position feeling like you partied like it's 1999 even though you fell asleep at 8:30 watching HGTV? Does the very smell of garlic cooking or someone's should-be-illegal-in-all-fifty-states Drakkar Noir make you want to toss your Wheaties? It's time to take a deep breath, put your feet up, and Paddy O'Preggo it, my friend!

makes 1 serving

6 ounces chilled Sprite
Fresh lime juice
1 scoop lime sherbet

Pour the Sprite into a tall glass. Squeeze in lime juice to taste. Add a scoop of lime sherbet to the top. Serve with a straw, float style.

Modest Madras

Any modesty you cling to up until the moment of childbirth will fly out the window once it's showtime. During my first delivery, after ~~a cajillion~~ several hours of pushing and an epidural that subsequent deliveries led me to believe might have been a placebo, I would've let the janitor see me buck nekkid if it meant the baby would come. (I will die asserting that the epidural meds were bought on eBay from China and were therefore counterfeit. Make sure you demand the good $hit.)

So when you get to that point in your pregnancy where you'd rather listen to Air Supply on repeat than bend down to tie your own shoes—that's when it's time to let go. For me, the day came when I asked hubs to shave my legs. If your hubs tries to say he doesn't know how to do legs, just point to his scratchy face and say, "Bitch, no. You can and you will!" (You can also save that line for a few years later, when you tell him it's his up to take Junior to the party at Chuck E. Cheese. For better or worse, people!)

makes 1 serving

Ice

3 ounces chilled cranberry juice

2 ounces chilled orange juice

Orange wheel, for garnish

Fill a tall glass with ice, pour the juices over, and stir. Garnish with an orange wheel.

Couchy Creamsicle®

After I delivered my second baby, the hubs, doctor, and nurses were all, "WHOA!" and started whooping it up. Turns out he was almost ten (ten!) pounds. The veteran nurse shrieked, "That's what we get for feeding mamas all those prenatal vitamins nowadays!" (Seriously. Back when moms-to-be were chasing their cigarettes with whiskey, babies were never that big.)

Suddenly, the few weeks leading up to his birth made more sense. I was splayed out on the couch at night uttering niceties like, "There's no blankity-blank dinner because I can't move!" Shuffling to the fridge was a chore. So imagine my surprise when I learned that a woman ran a marathon, had lunch, and gave birth afterward. A mar-a-freaking-thon. 26.2 MILES. Not 26.2 steps, which I whined about when I was nine months pregnant.

I want to put an asterisk after her name:

Nine-month baby mama marathoner*

(*Results not typical. Please don't try this at home.)

Yay for her, but duuuuude. She's gonna ruin it for the restuvus! It's like a diet—some can pull it off, but most will fail. Results.not.typical.

I'm just repeating what I hear.

Now ring for the hubs to make up a batch of Couchy Creamsicles!

makes 16 servings

½ gallon orange sherbet

½ gallon vanilla ice cream

2 quarts chilled orange juice

2 liters chilled ginger ale

In batches, blend together the sherbet, ice cream, and OJ. Pour into a punch bowl or other large serving container. Pour in the ginger ale last to make fizz.

CHAPTER TWO

Baby

Woohoo—you did it! ~~Drugs rule~~. I knew you could! You have your baby. Um, now what? First, do not panic. You are smart! You are ready! You have elastic-waist pants! You have resources ... your friends, your relatives, your pediatrician, ~~this book, Facebook, and a liquor cabinet~~. And remember, if you're having a bad day and are worried that you're not doing this parenting thing right, just think, dumb people have kids, too—and they manage. Ta da! You'll be fiiiiine. Use your instincts, buckle up, and put your big girl pants on—it's the ride of your life.

Fatty McSchlumpy

When you're pregnant, big is beautiful. Birds sing, doors open, skin glows. When you're not pregnant, big is you swallowed a Twinkie factory, you hold your own damn door open with your back fat, and birds stop in midflight and stare. See, there's a fine line between pregnancy and fat: childbirth. One minute you're pregnant, and the next the baby's out and you're just … fat.

Oh, there's a grace period. Right out of the gate, when everyone knows you just had a baby, it's like you're fat* with an asterisk (*But she just had a baaaby! Considering she just had a baaaby, she looks good!*). After a few months of that, you're just a garden-variety fatty who hasn't lost the weight—the schlumpy "before" in the weight-loss ad. You might score a sympathetic look if you're lugging your new baby around, but if caught out alone, for-get-it.

I admit it. It bothered me when even the Wii Fit beatch called me fat a few months post-pregnancy. But so what if we have a little more junk in the trunk. It's a small price to pay for life's best gift, a baby.

makes 1 or 2 servings

4 ounces (½ cup) cream of coconut

2 ounces Kahlúa

1 ounce black rum

1 ounce crème de cacao

4 ounces (½ cup) heavy cream

2 cups ice

Blend all ingredients together to the desired consistency. Share with a friend to cut the calories (or not).

Muffintopmommy Mudslide

I've sorta had a muffin top since third grade. Some girls got boobs in the third grade. I got a muffin top. Ain't genetics a bitch?

Pregnancy didn't help. No matter what shape or size you were pre-pregnancy, even when you've "lost the weight," stuff just isn't where you left it. (And if it is? I'm just not sure we can be friends.)

At some point post-baby, you'll have to go somewhere that requires an outfit nicer than a spit-up-stained shirt and yoga pants. If you're like me, you make a frantic dash to the store, try on everything, hate everything, and come home with the dreaded muffin-top restrictor undergarment.

But if you don a garment that reduces your muffin top and whittles your waist, where does the muffin top go? Truth? It comes out your underarms and your tush. And when you take off said undergarment, it's like opening up a tube of crescent rolls—POP! Look out, thar she blows!

Let's just ditch that sucker and have a mudslide instead!

makes 1 serving

¾ ounce vanilla Stolichnaya vodka

¾ ounce Kahlúa

¾ ounce Baileys Irish Cream

½ ounce half-and-half

Big squirt of chocolate syrup

Ice

Whipped cream, for garnish

Shake the vodka, Kahlúa, Baileys, half-and-half, and chocolate syrup with ice, strain into a chilled martini glass, and top with whipped cream.

Colicky Cider

When my oldest was born, he cried and he cried and he cried. Then I cried. All day long. For several months. The doctor said he "just had colic" and we'd have to ride it out. I felt guilty (welcome to motherhood; mother = guilt) because even though I couldn't love him more, I was all, "Seriously? Is this your game plan? Cry till my brain bleeds?"

I remember the hubs coming home one night and me just muttering, "There's no dinner." This smart man—who is clearly into self-preservation—said, "No problem," and suggested I get out of the house and pick something up. I moved so fast there was a plume of Road Runner smoke behind me. Chubs can move, yo! I made sure to hit the sub shop with the liquor license and enjoyed every sip of a beer by myself while I waited for our food in silence.

If you have a colicky baby, I promise one day you'll hear the silence and realize the crying has stopped. And then? It's cause to celebrate with the friends and family who helped you through it with this yummy concoction. (Unless you'd rather party solo at the sub shop?)

makes 16 servings

2 (750 ml) bottles chilled white wine

32 ounces (4 cups) chilled pomegranate juice

16 to 32 ounces (2 to 4 cups) Captain Morgan Spiced Rum

½ gallon chilled apple cider

A few apples, thinly sliced

Brown sugar and cinnamon, for rimming the glasses

Add the wine, juice, rum (to your liking), cider, and apple slices to a large (2-gallon) drink container, stir, and chill for at least 2 hours.

Serve in rocks glasses or martini glasses rimmed with a mixture of 3 parts brown sugar to 1 part cinnamon.

Long Drivin' Iced Tea

Road trips used to mean flying by the seat of your pants, hoping you had enough Twizzlers, gas money, and mix tapes to get you where you were going. No schedules, no stress, and laughing till you cried playing name games and mocking the local scenery. The worst that happened was a flat tire or a traffic ticket. ("You were pleasure cruising!" the judge scolded my BF, back in college.)

Now? Road trips mean 15 tons of diapers, wipes, and snacks weighing down the loser cruiser, with kids squawking in the back. Fun! As for the Twizzlers? Nooo! You can't let your kids see you eat those, or they'll want some, too. Turning the bus into a sugar shack is a rookie mistake. Laughing till you cry? Absolutely. Just hold the laughing. A mix tape? I think that's called an iPod Shuffle now, but whatever—you won't hear it over the screeching anyway.

At least you'll never get a traffic ticket. If an officer pulls you over, most of his five senses will be so insulted that he'll sprint for the safety of his car, screaming, "Just go, you poor bastards!" Quota? What quota?

Score! Take that, judge.

makes 1 serving

½ ounce vodka	*1 ounce sweet-and-sour mix*
½ ounce gold tequila	*Ice*
½ ounce rum	*2 ounces Coca-Cola*
½ ounce gin	*1 lemon wedge, for garnish*
½ ounce triple sec	

Shake the liquor and sweet-and-sour mix with ice. Strain into a tall glass filled with ice, and add a splash of Coke. Garnish with a lemon wedge.

Banana Baby Brain

Why didn't anyone tell me having a baby lowers your IQ? I might've tried to save up more brain cells. (I'm beginning to wonder if the Beer Pong Championship of 1993 was really worth it.) I've driven off with my phone on the hood of my car, not noticing until it went airborne. I've left the garden hose on … for eight hours. Mo' Nature, mea culpa, I know not what I do.

But bolting out of bed one night at 3 a.m. realizing I forgot to pay the cable bill—that's most concerning. Because where would I be without Matt Lauer in the morning? Who else would I have coffee with? Baby doesn't care about pressing issues like what's going on in the Middle East and which jeans are right for my body type (die, skinny jeans, die!). And as much as I love to spend my nights reading and writing, I do love me some Jersey housewives. Watching those cat fights makes me realize I don't need therapy after all—I can just have a drink and watch the madness ensue. If a phone has to die in the process and the earth runs dry, it's a small price to pay for my sanity.

makes 1 serving

1½ ounces coconut rum

¼ ounce lime juice

1 teaspoon sugar

1 banana

Lime wedge, for garnish

Blend all ingredients in a blender until smooth. Serve in a glass and garnish with a lime wedge.

Spit 'Em Up Sour

All babies spit up. But some hurl a day's worth of formula straight up into the air, geyser style.

I had that baby. And I have the carpets and furniture to prove it. No man, woman, or child within four feet of this baby was safe. Many costume changes went down during this unfortunate period. Some days, when the bitter smell of spit-up graced my shoulder, I gave up and didn't even bother changing. I figured it was just part of the gig.

Still, while on a rare escape out for cocktails with girlfriends, I happened to look down at my black shoe and notice it was splattered with white spit-up, and I wondered how I got to this place. I used to be a buttoned-up, ~~semi~~ styling gal, who paid close attention to grooming. So when my friend gently told me white stuff also adorned the back of my shirt, I decided I was going down swinging. I knew this was a moment to soldier on—because when you manage to get out on a rare furlough, grooming be damned. Spit up or shut up; unless the bar is on fire, don't you dare go home early!

makes 1 serving

3 ounces whiskey	*Ice*
1 ounce fresh lemon juice	*Maraschino cherry, for garnish (optional)*
½ teaspoon sugar	

Shake the whiskey, lemon juice, and sugar well with ice. Strain into a rocks glass filled with ice. Garnish with a cherry, if desired.

Sleeptastic Sangria

Now I understand why the military employs sleep deprivation as a tactic to extract intel from enemies. I contend (with my English degree and complete lack of scientific evidence) that it's physiologically impossible to function safely and think clearly on a few hours of sleep coupled with vats of coffee for weeks on end. Never mind the ridiculous television programming that I found myself watching to stay awake while feeding my babes (RIP, Billy Mays—OxiClean really does whiten brights and brighten whites … wait, what?), or that the bags under my eyes are very unbecoming and led me to make very costly and rash decisions at the Clinique counter. So I have to tell you, after several months of getting up with a newborn every few hours to feed, I would have totally sold my soul to the highest bidder for a full night of sleep … and I wouldn't need no fancy 400-thread-count sheets. Recliner, park bench—hell, even a dog bed would do. Move over, Fido—and you'd better not snore.

makes 6 servings

1 (750 ml) bottle chilled dry red wine

24 ounces chilled sparkling lemonade

1 teaspoon sugar

Any combination of orange, lemon, lime, and apple slices

Ice

In a pitcher, stir together the wine, lemonade, and sugar. Add the fruit—whatever you prefer. Serve chilled over ice.

Cheesy Sea Breezy

Since you have the cutest baby who ever drooled, you're going to want lots of pictures—for you, family, friends, neighbors, and everyone else who you're sure adores your chunky cherub. It's not like when I was a kid. My mom trimmed my bangs—with the same scissors she probably opened cardboard boxes with. (Yeah, um, as it turns out, it's not as easy as it looks.) She dressed me in my finest bad plaid, brought me to the local department store, plunked me down on the avocado green shag carpet in front of a fake-looking lake scene, told me to smile, and snap, snap, it was over.

I'm not busting on my mom—it was the '70s; that was how parents rolled. But be prepared. The photo shoot of today is not child's play. Bring your game face or go home. You'd better come armed with costume changes, extra diapers, and props. You need to be ready to make a complete arse out of yourself trying to get your baby to "perform." The photo shoot is when you realize that the baby has all the power. And you? You'll be dripping sweat by the time it's over. Thirsty? Say cheese … puhleeease.

makes 1 serving

2 ounces vodka

3 ounces chilled grapefruit juice

2 ounces chilled cranberry juice

Ice

Grapefruit wedge, for garnish

Shake everything together with ice. Strain into a highball glass filled with ice. Garnish with a grapefruit wedge.

Five-Alarm 529

Instant heartburn: If you have a baby now, it'll cost you up to a half million bucks to raise the little darling and put him or her through a public college— more if you go private. And you'd better hope you don't have a Doogie Howser on your hands, because that'll give you even less time to save. And an Ivy Leaguer? Sure, everyone would love to say, "My little Thurston is off to Hahhhvahd!" But if little Thurston doesn't have a trust fund or a scholarship, good luck.

Breathe with me now … I'm no mathlete, but it didn't take long to figure out that with three kids, there's no way hubs and I could possibly put enough money in their 529 plans to totally pay for college. I'm hoping to help as much as I can, and I'm also hoping that when they graduate and make it big someday, they'll pay for the fancy assisted living with the open bar and casino field trips for mama. A girl can dream. Until then, bring on the heartburn.

makes 1 serving

2 ounces Captain Morgan Spiced Rum

6 ounces (¾ cup) chilled ginger ale

Ice

Lime wheel, for garnish

Pour the rum over ice in a highball glass, then add the ginger ale. Garnish with a lime wheel.

Klepto Kahlúa

It's not cool to use your baby to steal. But the second you walk into a store with your baby in a car seat in the cart, you're at risk. Either you practically forget that your bundle is there because the little angel is snoozing, or she's squawking because she's hungry, thirsty, blowing out her diaper, or just wants to be a pain in the arse because she already knows she can. (That sound? It should be piped into prisons. I guarantee repeat offenders would be scared straight. You're welcome, criminal justice system.)

Last time, I got the squawking baby and shopped in a distracted state. Forget that I went in for toilet paper and left with $100 of who knows what. I got all the way to the car and realized that a ChapStick (I might be an addict) and a bag of chocolates (don't judge me) were wedged between the car seat and the side of the cart. Begrudgingly, I schlepped back into the store to pay. Hey, if I'm gonna sully my ~~relatively~~ good name, I'm going for the big haul, not some $3 ChapStick. Besides, I don't want to wind up in prison with screaming-baby sounds piped into my cell!

makes 1 serving

½ ounce Kahlúa

½ ounce Grand Marnier

½ ounce Baileys Irish Cream

8 ounces (1 cup) hot coffee

Whipped cream, for garnish (optional)

Pour the Kahlúa, Grand Marnier, and Baileys into a mug. Add the hot coffee. Top with whipped cream, if desired.

Houdini Hurricane

What loving, smart parent wouldn't baby-proof their home? I fully admit that I'm ~~totally~~ slightly neurotic. My kids had special crib sheets that covered the entire front and back of the mattress because I feared they'd get tangled in a regular one and not be able to breathe. (I know. I know!) My outlet covers are plugged. My blind cords are strung up. My cabinet full of household chemicals, locked. My windows open from the top.

You think your house is all baby-proofed, when Houdini baby proves he's already faster and trickier than you. There you'll be, with a house full of adults over in your baby bubble, yet no one notices baby teetering at the top of the ungated stairs, and boom! Rolls down like a little burrito, thud, thud, thud, until he lands at the bottom, the whole time inches from your grasp. (Yes, this happened to me. Thankfully he was okay—the houseful of adults, not so much.) Remember to always expect the unexpected. Accidents may happen despite our best efforts. And when they do … this hurricane is for you!

makes 1 serving

1 ounce white rum

1 ounce dark rum

1 ounce Bacardi 151 rum

4 ounces (½ cup) chilled orange juice

4 ounces (½ cup) chilled pineapple juice

Ice

Splash of grenadine

Orange wheel, for garnish

Shake the rums and juices with ice. Strain into a hurricane glass filled with ice. Add a splash of grenadine to the top. Garnish with an orange wheel.

Frogger

Once you finally deliver your baby, the next few days are a complete blur of feedings, burpings, and awesomesauce nurses being on hand to help you with everything. After the VIP treatment, you get bounced out of the hospital within forty-eight hours with the loveliest of parting gifts: your baby. (And what's left of your body. Hint: Baby won't be the only one in diapers. Don't shoot the messenger!)

The real fun begins on the car ride home. Why does no one talk about this? I'm just gonna say it: Even if you live only a few miles from the hospital, it will seem like the longest car ride of your life. After gingerly handling baby like a piece of fine china for two days with trained medical professionals at the ready, you're hovering over your tiny bundle ensconced in his car seat, feeling like every bump in the road might snap his little neck.

Once you survive the inaugural car ride and arrive home sweating, feeling every bit like a human Frogger, it's so on. (You can totally do this! Let's review: Even dumb people have kids!)

makes 1 serving

1½ ounces gin   *Ice*

½ ounce Midori melon liqueur   *2 ounces champagne*

½ ounce fresh sour mix

Shake the gin, Midori, and sour mix with ice. Strain into a rocks glass with ice and splash with champagne.

Scary Shotty

Even though you might feel like you're sleepwalking when you get home with your new baby, I swear you'll be strangely alert as you care for your bundle around the clock. Before you know it, it's time to take baby for his first doctor's visit. After you dress him in forty-two layers (so what if it's mid-July … you don't want baby to catch a chill!) and make a valiant effort to shield him from Typhoid Mary in the waiting room, it's game time.

The appointment is all standard stuff. The doctor will ask you how the delivery went, how you're doing, how baby is eating, sleeping, etc. Hopefully you'll be coherent—they don't expect you to be at your most poised. But toward the end, all you'll hear is, "Blabbity, blah, blah," because with burning eyes and a foggy head, you'll be trying to focus, but all you'll see are gigundo needles closing in on your teeny new baby.

Baby howls; you sob. Baby gets Tylenol. But what about mama? It hurts us just as much! Good lord, a mama can take only so much stress in a period of just a few days. And you still have another car ride to get through!

makes 1 serving

Shot of limoncello (keep bottle in freezer)

Pour the cold limoncello into the chilled shot glass. Sip and enjoy!

CHAPTER THREE

Toddler

Do you like sitting down? That's too bad, because you won't get to unless you're indisposed, and even then, you'll have an uninvited guest lurking in the loo. If you don't have nerves of steel to begin with, you will once you're mom to a toddler. Whether they're teetering on top of a chair, trying to reach something that could maim them; flailing on the ground over a perceived injustice, like you offering them the wrong cereal; or showing off their new PG-13 vocabulary in the deli line, you need to play some mean D. It's exhausting. But don't worry. Their chubby cheeks and impish grins are guaranteed to keep you from running away from home. And besides, some of their antics are crazy funny. Especially to everyone else. Good luck!

Princey Plumber

The other morning, I'd just gotten my first-grader on the bus, and was standing in my kitchen enjoying my coffee with Matt. (Lauer. Remember? We're tight. Sometimes I also have a cup later in the day with Ellen. We dance. We sing.) My four-year-old interrupts, booming, "Done pooping!" from the bathroom. Sighing, I shuffle into the bathroom to help him, and see mascara is smeared all over the wall, as he deadpans, "Oh, mom? He (pointing to two-year-old splayed out on the floor) flushed your makeup stick."

Of course he did. Because that's so fun.

First, I'm convinced there's a conspiracy to make me look like the haggard hausfrau I feel like some days, when little people flush the only ingredients I have to make myself look alive. Second, this isn't the first item that's been sucked down where the sun don't shine. Matchbox cars, Lego pieces, tampons (which, FYI, are also known as fishing poles) all met an untimely demise.

So let me give you one piece of advice I wish I'd heeded when I began having kids: You need to get jiggy with a plumber. Find a good one, commit his phone number to memory, and treat him like the prince he is!

makes 1 serving

4 ounces (½ cup) chilled lemonade

2 ounces raspberry vodka

Splash of fresh lime juice

Stir together the lemonade and vodka. Pour over ice in a tall glass or Mason jar. Splash with lime juice to taste.

Golden Nugget

I'm rolling with the shorties one day and two-year-old is screaming "Shipping Off to Boston" at the top of his lungs. It's a symptom of a third child … we shot right past Laurie Berkner straight to Dropkick Murphys, Jimmy Buffett, and Sir Mix-a-Lot. (Just don't—he's a musical genius.)

I smile as I glance in the rearview mirror, when I notice he's crooning with his mouth full. I'm about to scold him for singing with food in his mouth, when I realize I haven't given him anything to eat. Wait. a. second. It's a chicken nugget. The last time we had those was … uh oh.

I always joke that if our car ever breaks down in the middle of nowhere we can just live in it until help arrives. There are probably a half dozen coats to keep us warm, books and toys to entertain us, and enough Goldfish, fries, and petrified nuggets on the floor to sustain us indefinitely.

Mmm. E. coli. It's what's for lunch!

(Laurie Berkner and fresh food are for firstborns. After that, it's suburban survival of the fittest.)

makes 1 serving

1½ ounces gold tequila

2 ounces chilled cranberry juice

¾ ounce triple sec

3 ounces chilled sweet-and-sour mix

Ice

Lime wheel, for garnish

Shake the tequila, juice, triple sec, and sweet-and-sour mix with ice, and strain into a rocks glass filled with ice. Garnish with a lime wheel.

Markerita

I totally hate to be an I-told-you-so, because glass houses and all that shizzy, but there's a reason why I never tried the much touted "quiet time" after my kids ditched their naps. Yes, I'm sure it works for many moms, and I trust you'll have the instincts to know if you can pull it off with your kids. Don't ever forget: You know your own child better than anyone.

I know my kids. I knew that if mine were left unattended but awake (let that term marinate for a sec … unattended but awake!) they'd manage to MacGyver their way into nuthin' good. As it is, they always manage to find the one outlet I forgot to cover. The last time it happened, my two-year-old grabbed my keys and tried to stick them in the socket—yes, yes he did. Who DOES that? My kids. Who should not be left alone. In the quiet. Ever. Quiet = bad.

Not every quiet situation amounts to danger, but it often means a bunch of no-good nonsense guaranteed to induce pain and suffering—for you. Example? The time my friend's son crawled into his little sister's crib and "Sharpied" her from head to toe. That? Is what I'm talking about. No. Just … no.

makes 4 servings

6-ounce can frozen limeade concentrate

5 to 6 ounces tequila (to your taste)

2 ounces triple sec

Splash of orange juice

Squeeze of fresh lime juice

Handful of ice cubes

Fill a blender with the ingredients. Blend until smooth.

Crankasaurus de Cocoa

Let's talk about people whose kids still nap in kindergarten. I just can't wrap my head around how they get their kids to go the (insert bad word) to sleep at bedtime. If my kids conk out in the car too late in the afternoon, we're guaranteed to crash and burn at bedtime. Not good—you know that's when I hang with the Jersey housewives (I need a stylist. Where can I get me some chinchilla?), read about pressing issues of today in ~~People~~ Newsweek, and ~~blog about my muffin top~~ write important social commentary.

I'm sure parents of older nappers are wonderful people who floss regularly and wouldn't cut me in the carpool line, so I try to stay open-minded and like them. I'm not a hater. But see, my kids all gave their naps up early, the youngest one before he turned two. So that makes mama and offspring morph into total crankasauruses come 5 o'clock some days. So if you come near me a moment too close to the witching hour and lament that your four-year-old napped for only forty-five minutes, please be advised that you won't see the muffin top coming when you hit the deck. Cheers!

makes 1 serving

Mug of hot cocoa

1½ ounces Smirnoff Fluffed Marshmallow Vodka

Dollop of whipped cream

Shaved chocolate, for garnish (optional)

Prepare a mug of hot cocoa as directed. Stir in vodka, top with whipped cream, and add shaved chocolate to the top for a prettier presentation, if desired.

Emergentini

Being a parent is scary. One week you're just a woman who can't see her feet and a dude going on late-night ice cream runs, and the next you're parents teetering on the curb of the hospital with a tiny baby and no instruction manual. You get instructions with a toaster. (And shouldn't toasting things be kinda intuitive? Duh.) With a kid, nada. You quickly realize that even when you have the best of intentions to do everything right, parenting isn't black and white. Even when you do your best for your child, it's not always good enough.

On the parenting scale of frightening stuff, there's nothing scarier than a trip to the emergency room. We've had two trips for stitches, a direct hit to the eye with OxiClean, and a tumble down the stairs. Inserting the world's loudest PHEW, they've all been okay. (Side note: I'd like to thank the good people of Social Services for realizing that I am, indeed, a fit parent.)

If you wind up at the ER, I wish you all the luck. And vodka. But most of all the ability to forgive yourself, because most likely, you'll be feeling more pain than your child.

makes 1 serving

2 ounces vodka	*Ice*
1 teaspoon dry vermouth	*Stuffed green olive*

Add the vodka and vermouth to an ice-filled shaker. Shake vigorously. (Or just hold it—you'll be shaking anyway!) Strain into a chilled martini glass. Drop an olive into the glass.

No!Jito

"No" is never just a simple word as far as a toddler's concerned, especially when someone else is around, like a grandmother or a friend. You tell the little scamps no and they seem to dig their heels in even deeper. It's as though they smell fear ...

"We have company? Da da da! SHOWTIME!"

"Please stop trying to swing from the chandelier."

"NO!"

"Please stop dancing on the table."

"NO!"

"Please don't call every man you see inside Home Depot 'Daddy'!"

"NO!"

Nonononono. And when a toddler tells you no, they are ad-a-mant. But when you tell them no, they think it's a relative term, subject to debate and incessant questions.

"No, you may not play in traffic."

"Why?"

"Because you could get hit by a car."

"Why?"

"Because people drive too fast."

"Why?"

"Because they're in too much of a hurry."

"Why?"

"Because they're STUPID!"

"You said STUP-ID! You said STUP-ID!"

"No, no, I didn't."

"YES, you did!"

I win, I win, I win—I got him to say yes!

makes 1 serving

8 to 10 fresh mint leaves

4 lime wedges or 4 ounces (½ cup) fresh lime juice

2 tablespoons white superfine sugar

1½ ounces white rum

Ice

4 ounces (½ cup) chilled club soda

Lime wheel, for garnish

In a cocktail shaker, muddle together the mint leaves, lime wedges or juice, sugar, and rum. Add a cup of ice, pour in the club soda, and shake. Strain into a tall Collins glass filled with ice. Garnish with a lime wheel.

Harvey Wallpainter

It's family folklore that my brother crayoned in black all over a freshly painted wall back in the early '70s, that unfortunate time period when hair was bad and crayons weren't washable. Cursing ensued, and the wall was repainted. Can I get a woot woot for the cat who invented washable markers and crayons? This Harvey Wallpainter is in your honor, you genius, you.

See, it never fails—the minute you turn your head to answer the ringing phone or sign for the UPS package (New shoes? Squee!), some hooligan is swiping his crayon all over the wall like a budding Monet. And if by chance your kids get their retro on with the few renegade unwashable crayons that infiltrate the house from a restaurant or goody bag—they should really call them no-good bags, if you ask me—then just make it a double. Trust me, you'll be busy all night long working it off, painting.

makes 1 serving

1½ ounces vodka

4 ounces (½ cup) chilled orange juice

¾ ounce Galliano

Ice

Orange wheel, for garnish

Stir together vodka, orange juice, and Galliano in a rocks glass with ice. Garnish with an orange wheel.

Shitzer Spritzer

When you know your kid is old enough to be potty trained, but he won't, he might as well shout, "I've got the pow-ah, and I'll pee when I want to in my comfy, stay-dry, made-too-damn-well diapies, which cost 25 percent of the household budget. And P.S. environment, too bad for you, too!"

There are people who inexplicably get their kids potty trained when they're barely two. I'm unaware of the methods they use, but I harbor suspicions that they might not be on the up and up. Lest I feel like an utter failure for wiping the bums of children who are old enough to articulate in paragraph form that they need a fresh diaper, let's just assume that these parents are up to no good. Or that they have some awesome secret they ain't letting us in on. Why do I picture them sitting with their feet up sipping chardonnay while their kids wipe their own bums?

As for the rest of us tree-killin', budget-busting schlubs? We can have a drink too, dammit, but we'll water ours down with club soda, since we're still buying diapers. Still yummy. So there.

makes 1 serving

4 ounces chilled white wine
2 ounces chilled club soda

Squeeze of fresh lemon or lime juice
Ice

Stir together the wine, club soda, and lemon or lime juice, and pour over ice in a wine glass or rocks glass.

Cosmopotty

Did you say potty trained? I'll drink to that. Except when I won't. Sometimes I think it's easier to have a kid in diapers.

Picture this. You're out with the fam at the finest two-and-a-half-star restaurant in town. Bad restaurants do happen to good people. Nobody fries cheese like this place, I'm telling you. Your deliciously mediocre food arrives, and you manage to cut up the kids' food into eleventy billion pieces and take one bite of your almost still hot food, when a little voice chirps from beyond the ketchup, "I have to go potty!"

"Me too! I have to go too!"

"I wanna come too! Not fair that he gets to go and I don't!"

Sister, don't even tell me you don't fleetingly wish he could've just taken a silent whiz in a diaper.

Garçon? I'll have another. Hubs is driving the bus home tonight!

makes 1 serving

1½ ounces vodka

1½ ounces chilled cranberry juice

¾ ounce triple sec

½ ounce sweetened lime juice, such as Rose's

Ice

Lime wheel, for garnish

Shake the vodka, cranberry juice, triple sec, and sweetened lime juice with ice, strain into a chilled martini glass, and garnish with a lime wheel.

Beerios

It's 5 p.m. Your house looks like a stage-5 hurricane ripped through it. Everyone is screaming. Or crying. Or screaming crying. Your eyes land on the Pottery Barn catalog, where children calmly sit in playrooms nicer than your home. They color on paper—not the walls. The mom has no muffin top. No junk in the trunk. Varicose veins? Um, no.

You need a mental break, so you hop on Facebook, hoping desperately for something, anything to lift you from your own temporary madness. Instead, you're on long enough to see that your childhood nemesis is in killer shape, is wealthy and aging well, and has a tremendous career. Bitch, no! She probably flies first class and doesn't buy her clothes in a red cart with her Market Pantry snack treats.

Your seething is interrupted when toddler swipes the warehouse-sized Cheerios bag, squealing as he trips, while Cheerios rain down everywhere. Don't get your granny panties in a twist—beer-thirty is on! All is right with the world. (First class ain't what it used to be anyway. At least, so I'm told.)

makes 1 serving

1 (12-ounce) bottle cold beer
Market Pantry chips (optional)

Freeze a beer mug for at least 30 minutes. Pour beer into frosty mug. Repeat if necessary. Serve with Market Pantry chips, if you really want to get all crazy.

Mother Clucker Coffee

I wanted to like him. His return symbolized the end of another winter living in black and white. His presence gave us permission to pack away the salty boots and Puffalump jackets. But he started coming around earlier and earlier. He got louder. Prouder. He acted like he owned the joint. And then? He woke the two-year-old at 4:55 a.m. Eastern. Standard. Time. (Otherwise known as … the time zone in which we live.) Bad, bad birdie. YOU LITTLE MOTHER CLUCKER! You don't mess with the Mother Hen!

Is it bad form to try to fight a bird? Is there a law against trying to shoot one with a Nerf gun? I love animals. I do. Nature … yay! I'm all for it. But seriously. How many times can you wake a house full of little kids before mama winds up getting foul with the fowl? Audubon Society, SOS!

makes 1 serving

1½ ounces Baileys Irish Cream
8 ounces (1 cup) hot coffee
Whipped cream, for topping

Stir Irish cream into a mug of coffee and top with whipped cream.

Bloody Binky!

Regret, thy name is Binky. I regret I ever let the hospital nursery put that bloody Binky into my son's mouth. (Enablers!) Because he wound up being a Binky psycho.

I mean ... Binky? What Binky? My walkin', talkin' two-year-old doesn't use one of those! I don't (often) Marine-crawl at warp speed in the dark of night searching fruitlessly for a dropped Binky under the crib! Do you?

Where is that brickin' finkie?!

Don't even lie—I saw the lump on your head where you hit it on the bottom of the crib. Amateur! And it's never a good sign if your child can come up to you and demand his Binky in fluent English, telling you which one he prefers and where you can locate it.

No need to hang your head in shame. We all know—this is a safe place. And hey, if your kid can enjoy his bloody Binky, you should, too!

makes 1 serving

1½ ounces vodka	*Dash black pepper*
1 teaspoon horseradish	*Ice*
¼ ounce fresh lemon juice	*4 ounces (½ cup) V-8 juice*
6 dashes Worcestershire sauce	*Celery stalk, for garnish*
2 dashes Tabasco sauce (or to taste)	

Place the vodka, horseradish, lemon juice, Worcestershire and Tabasco sauces, and pepper in a tall glass with ice. Top with V-8 juice. Stir. Top with pepper and garnish with the celery stalk.

Sour Sib

"He goes back to hostiple! Now!" my friend's daughter demanded, stabbing the air toward the object of her derision, her new baby brother.

"He's not going back to the hospital, sweetie. He lives here now. You get to be the BIG sister."

"NO! You go downstairs, baby!"

(She knew that's where unwanted things went ... the trash, the treadmill, mommy's cookbooks, daddy's skin-tight high school hockey jersey from the glory days.)

"His name is Matthew, and he's not going downstairs. Mommy needs you to help me with him because you're so BIG! Won't that be fun?"

"NO! I thirsty!" Saucy toddler swoops in, grabs baby's bottle, and defiantly takes a swig.

My friend was growing increasingly exasperated with her toddler acting out, until another friend asked her, "Why are we surprised a toddler acts out when we bring home a new baby? How would you like it if your husband brought home a new woman and said, 'She'll be living here with us and I love her just as much as you! Deal!"

Ummmm ... point taken.

makes 1 serving

**Sugar, for rimming the glass
(optional)**

Ice

2 ounces vodka

**6 ounces (¾ cup) chilled
lemonade**

Lemon wheel, for garnish

Rim a tall glass with sugar, if desired, and fill with ice. Shake the vodka and lemonade with ice, and strain into the glass. Garnish with a lemon wheel.

Scary Santa

If you celebrate Christmas, buckle up. Nothing says Christmas cheer like dolling the kid up to wait in what looks to be a bread line in Communist Russia to see Santa. If you survive the sojourn and make it to the front, you'll realize that the jolly man in the big red suit is pretty freaking scary to small kids. Seriously. Our Santa's face was redder than his suit, and he boomed, "Come sit on my lap, handsome little boy!" to my son in the most scary-ass boozy Deliverance accent. What is even remotely right about that? (And don't even get me started on the inbred-looking elves.)

You soon realize you don't know whose lap you're dumping your kid on. It seemed a lot like stranger danger to me, and I was putting my poor, innocent kid up to it. Just a wrongity wrong mess of wrongness. I'm hoping Santa was just into the eggnog too much that night and not recently released from the chain gang, but I dunno …

makes 1 serving

2 ounces vanilla vodka

2 ounces amaretto

2 ounces half-and-half

Ice

Dash of unsweetened cocoa powder (optional)

Shake the vodka, amaretto, and half-and-half with ice and strain into a martini glass. Top with a dash of cocoa powder, if desired.

Mamakaze Bomb Drop

Being a mom to three boys, I got kind of haughty during their toddler years. I figured no other mom, especially my friends with girls, could possibly shock me with tales of over-the-top toddler antics.

My sons hung from the chandelier *for real* (who knew it wasn't just a figure of speech?). And somewhere around that calamitous stage when potty training began, all of them at one point or another dropped trou and peed on the carpet, on the sand at the beach (yay for beach day anonymity!), in the front yard (What's up, mail carrier!), and—although there's no proof, a mother just *knows*—hurled on command in front of company.

So I thought I had a lock on the grossest kid award. I'm not proud, just determined to succeed at this thing called motherhood—even if it means I'm the best failure on the block. Turns out, though, that two pristine girls I know pooped in the bathtub. During an actual bath. With siblings in the tub.

A potty party in the bathtub? A bomb drop? I'll drink to my loss. Cheers.

makes 1 serving

1½ ounces vodka

¾ ounce triple sec

½ ounce sweetened lime juice, such as Rose's

Ice

Lime wheel, for garnish

Shake the vodka, triple sec, and sweetened lime juice with ice, strain into a chilled martini glass, and garnish with a lime wheel.

Son of a Beach

It's sooo cute when all of a sudden your baby turns into a walking, talking little person. Hearing a tiny voice say "Mama" really is the "all" in all that. (Is too. Look it up on Wikipedia.) Before you know it, you'll forget about those sleepless nights. And varicose veins. And stretch marks. So what? You have a child prodigy! Scrap the college fund—you won't need it. Mama's gettin' a hot tub to soak her pretty veins. Huzzah!

Seemingly overnight, baby will have quite the vocabulary going. "Thank you," "Daddy," "Dunkin's"... that shorty is rollin'! And with a personality to match. You're all, "That's mah boy!" when he flirts with the cashier. Till you drop something and he hollers, "GOD DAMNIT!" in front of the 105-year-old bagger.

Now you're just a busted, wannabe, veiny hot tubber.

Son of a … beach.

makes 1 serving

1½ ounces vodka
¾ ounce peach schnapps
2 ounces chilled orange juice
2 ounces chilled cranberry juice
Ice

Shake the vodka, schnapps, and juices with ice. Strain into a rocks glass filled with ice.

Scarlet A

I took my kids for flu shots recently. Before I had time to wonder if they'd catch something nastier than the flu itself in the packed waiting room, four-year-old trips over his feet and goes airborne, breaking the fall with … the side of his face, just as two-year-old starts with some poor kid over a toy.

I tell him it's not his turn, but can barely hear myself think over four-year-old's wailing. I try to console four-year-old with hugs, as two-year-old continues to screech like Biff from *Back to the Future*, and I can *feel* everyone giving me "the eye." I've been found guilty by a jury of my waiting room peers of being the mother with no control over her tantrum toddler, as my face burns. Tough crowd.

Even the nurse was humorless. I don't even think GIs shipping off to World War II got shots administered that fast. She was probably thinking, "Take your sideshow and beat it, lady!" So when you feel like a Hester Prynne outcast—and it will happen—put the kids to bed and enjoy a Scarlet A!

makes 1 serving

2 ounces vodka

1 ounce Cointreau

½ ounce fresh lime juice

4 ounces (½ cup) chilled pomegranate juice

Ice

Lime twist, for garnish

Shake the vodka, Cointreau, and juices with ice and strain into a martini glass. Garnish with a lime twist.

CHAPTER FOUR

Preschool

Preschoolers. They're still up to no good, like they were when they were toddlers … but they're smarter about it. If you're not careful, you'll be shaking your head saying, "Wait, what? My three-and-a-half-year-old just punked me!" You might wish for a few minutes of quiet—but don't. Trust me. When it's too quiet, something is going down that's either dangerous or a hot mess of wrongity wrongness. The good news is, they're still cute enough to keep you coming back for more kisses. The bad news? They know it. (Insert laugh track here.)

Peach Snots

Never did I think my life would take me to a place where I'd actually catch throw-up in my hand or navigate diaper blowouts. I've done and seen things I don't care to describe in civilized social circles. (You're welcome.) Maybe I have post-traumatic stress disorder—I'm pretty sure I fit some of the criteria. If the men in white coats show up to take me away, I'll know things have really gone wrong.

But nothing prepared me for the day I stood in my best, clean Target duds, and my son rubbed his snotty nose on.my.shirt. Now who won't be invited to rock the Merona runway with the Tarjay models? One day you too can aspire to be a walking, talking, human Kleenex. (Friendly tip? I recommend washing in hot water!)

makes 1 serving

1½ ounces peach schnapps

1½ ounces vodka

4 ounces (½ cup) chilled cranberry juice

Ice

Splash of pineapple juice

Stir the schnapps, vodka, and cranberry juice in a rocks glass filled with ice. Splash pineapple juice over the top.

"TP" Tanqueray and Tonic

I figure I'll be wiping tushes until I'm collecting Social Security. I kid, I kid! (Not really.)

I have a two-year-old who I'm pretty sure will be going to college in Depends, because they won't make Diego Pull-Ups that are big enough. And though my preschooler is potty trained, he's content to finish his biz by screeching, "DONE POOOPING!" in tones that could wake the dead. (Translation: Come wipe my arse, beatch. And make it snappy.)

Pardon me while I shove a roll of Charmin where the sun doesn't shine. (My friends from high school and college are MDs and PhDs with second homes. I wipe bums.)

Live big with me!

makes 1 serving

Ice

2 ounces Tanqueray gin

4 ounces (½ cup) chilled tonic water

Squeeze of fresh lime juice

Lime wheel, for garnish

Fill a rocks glass with ice. Add the gin, tonic water, and lime juice, and stir. Garnish with a lime wheel.

Punkin Pansy

Remember Halloween costumes from back in the day? They came in a cheesy box with a clear cellophane front so you could see the mask. The mask barely covered your face, with tiny slits for the nose and eyes, and a thin elastic band to adhere it to your slippery face. Couple that with a flimsy, flammable polyester costume tied around your back, and you had a bunch of sweaty-faced kids stumbling around in the dark, breathing like a 1-900 hussy, who couldn't see for $hit, with no supervision.

But thank God the parents stayed home—a lot of 'rents smoked back then, and that surely would have spelled disaster. Stop, drop, and roll, kids!

Now? Costumes are made with fire-retardant materials, and masks facilitate age-appropriate breathing. Fancy treat bags hold the loot. Moms and dads stand watch while kids collect their candy—there are just as many parents as kids. What kind of punkin' pansies are we raising anyway?

I think we deserve a toast—for surviving our childhoods!

makes 1 serving

Brown sugar and cinnamon, for rimming the glass

1 (12-ounce) bottle pumpkin ale

1½ ounces vanilla vodka

Mix 3 parts brown sugar to 1 part cinnamon in a bowl or on a small plate. Rim a pint glass with the mixture. Pour the pumpkin ale into the glass and add the vanilla vodka.

Mouthy Muchacho

At some point during preschool, the inevitable potty talk commences. One of my boys started calling the other one "Poopoo diaper baby." Charming. And, thankfully, short-lived. It got worse before it got better, because then he went through a "stream of consciousness" phase—it was like Russian roulette. You never knew when or where he'd step on a landmine and belt out whatever came to mind. "That man has NO hair!" or the fan fave, "Boy, that is one biiiig lady!" and "Is there a baby in your belly?" (That one hurt. I had to put my foot down—he didn't get dessert that night.)

The worst part was that our two-year-old, who couldn't even speak that well or fully grasp the context of the potty talk, became guilty by association. One day at the store, an adorable girl squeaked, "Hi!" to him. Perched in the front of the shopping cart, he looked down at her and barked, "POO-POO!"

I bounced back with a Mouthy Muchacho. And started doing my shopping out of town. With dark glasses on. And a hat.

makes 1 serving

1 ounce tequila	*¼ ounce fresh lime juice*
1 ounce Grand Marnier	*Ice*
1½ ounces chilled orange juice	*Orange wheel, for garnish*

Shake the tequila, Grand Marnier, and juices with ice. Strain into a martini glass. Garnish with an orange wheel.

The Big Sloppowski

Why am I not a shareholder in a stain removal company? Between preschooler using his shirt as a napkin (my sincere regrets to Emily Post), drinks going airborne, and sticky yogurt landing on the floor, no surface is safe from my kids' sloppy reign. Paint from art class and sleeves soaked in their favorite food group, ketchup, round out the damage.

This isn't new, nor is it limited to boys. I remember my mama demanding to know why the fronts of my T-shirts were caked in dirt when I would come in from playing. (Remember when your mom would just open the back door and punt you out, and you wouldn't come back until dinner? No supervised playdates, no playrooms with seagrass rugs, chalkboards, and flat-screens with ginormous Elmos. If you got in a fight with another kid, you'd employ something called fight or flight. Let's just say I was not above belting a boy, cuz we all know I ain't fast.)

So I guess it shouldn't be shocking that I found it too laborious to walk around the fence to get to my neighbor's house—I just burrowed under the fence. Klassy!

How do you spell payback? The Big Sloppowski.

makes 1 serving

2 ounces Smirnoff Fluffed Marshmallow Vodka

2 ounces dark chocolate liqueur

2 ounces heavy cream

Marshmallow and shaved chocolate, for garnish (optional)

Stir the vodka, liqueur, and cream together in a rocks glass. Garnish with a marshmallow and shaved chocolate, if desired.

Separation Sour

Before my middle child started preschool, I might have boasted to the other parents that I'd be burning rubber out of the parking lot after drop-off the first morning. He'd been doing the drop-off/pickup drill with his older brother for two years, and always wanted to stay to play with the class. It got downright hard to drag him out of there toward the end of his brother's school year. He told everyone who would listen that he went to school before he was even enrolled.

So when he clung to my leg à la deer in the headlights that first morning, I got my smugguppance as the new parents tiptoed by me out of class. For the next few months, I had "that kid": first name, Cling, last name, Wrap. Eventually he realized circle time beat hanging with a thirtysomething muffin top, but not before emergency cocktails had to be employed on school nights. Heed my warning—kids are wildly unpredictable, so keep your mouth shut and your head down lest you be played the foo'!

makes 1 serving

Ice

1 ounce Midori melon liqueur

1 ounce whiskey sour mix

2 ounces chilled Sprite

Maraschino cherry, for garnish

Fill a highball glass with ice. Add the Midori, sour mix, and Sprite, and stir. Garnish with a cherry.

Penis Colada

With three boys, there are no awkward bath talks, because, well, they're all the same. Not so for my friend, who has boys and girls. When her son shot up out of the tub, pointing at his little sister, screaming, "IT FELL OFF! IT FELL OFF! MOOOOM! IT FELL OFF!" I really wish I had been there to hear my friend explain that, in fact, his sister's penis did not fall off, and that she'd be juuuuust fine without one. (Frankly, I do believe the sooner boys realize this, the better.)

Of course, every girl has her day, like the time I was going potty in a public bathroom stall with my three-year-old son, and he screeched, "Mommy, you go pee pee from your bum bum!" while a woman snickered in the next stall. Sister, if you're not gonna help me out, no laughing from the peanut gallery.

makes 1 serving

2 ounces light rum

3 ounces (⅓ cup) cream of coconut

6 ounces (¾ cup) chilled pineapple juice

1 cup ice

Maraschino cherry and/or pineapple slice, for garnish

Blend the rum, cream of coconut, pineapple juice, and ice until it is the desired consistency.

Serve in a tall glass, garnished with a cherry and/or pineapple slice.

Punchy Party Pants

Once preschool starts, it's party time. Pin the tail on the donkey in someone's backyard has been obliterated by ginormous birthday extravaganzas at bounce places, museums, and teddy bear factories. Color me guilty. I've thrown these parties for my own sons.

Think dozens of screeching preschoolers hopped up on sugar in an inflatable mosh pit. Fun! I contend party places are in collusion with the pharmaceutical industry, because these parties virtually ensure a migraine. Is it wrong that I wanna sucker-punch whoever started this $hit?

Maybe I'll just invite the other moms over for some Punchy Party Pants and an aspirin, and call it a day. (After I go through the no-good goody bags to confiscate the unwashable crayons and toys with lead paint that some poor kid probably made in China.) Gah!

makes 6 servings

1 (750 ml) bottle chilled champagne

4 ounces Cointreau

4 ounces brandy

4 ounces (½ cup) chilled carbonated water

Stir the ingredients together in a pitcher. Serve in martini glasses.

Big Flop Cupcake

You cook from scratch and get up to work out at 5 a.m. in your home that looks like a page out of *Better Homes and Gardens*? I won't sneer. In fact, I tip my muffin top to your discipline and mad skillz. But I just don't think I can bring myself to join you. See, I was happy to bask in my chubby mediocrity, until I found out two of my sons had peanut and nut allergies, making it next to impossible to find fun bakery birthday cakes that didn't say, "May contain peanuts/tree nuts." (Translation: May contain ingredients that could close my kids' throats and, thusly, kill them. No stress!)

So I resolved to get my Martha Stewart on. *For the children!* Enter Big Flop Cupcake. I tried to make a cupcake the size of my arse that looked like the awesomeness as *seen on TV*. I really did. But deep down, I knew I shouldn't have strayed from my number one girl, Betty (Crocker), and my trusty 12-count cupcake tin.

Vive la mediocrity! (Because saying it in half faux French somehow makes it feel that much less failure-ish.)

makes 1 serving

2 ounces Kahlúa

2 scoops vanilla ice cream

3 crushed Oreos

Blend all ingredients together until smooth. Serve in a parfait glass.

Sickie von Fluenberg

Moms aren't allowed to get sick.

Pre-kids? You felt awful, you called in sick. You lay around, got your *Judge Judy* on, and shuffled back to work the next day.

Now? Being sick is a total $hitshow. If you work, you probably used all your sick days to stay home when your kids were ill. And if you stay home, um, what sick days? You're totally at the mercy of the hub's schedule.

You can't exactly call a friend to come help either.

"Hi, I'm hurling like I went on a bender with Lindsay Lohan and want to crash on the bathroom floor. Can you come over to my germ festival and help my stanky ass?"

Yeah, no. You're on your own, sister.

That is when you realize this gig is 7 days a week, 24 hours a day, 365 days a year. Even prisoners get time off for good behavior! But moms? Moms need to boot and rally.

Your kids can eat cookies for breakfast, lunch, and dinner and watch 937 episodes of that whinybag Caillou, and provided they don't drink shoe polish or play with matches, you totally get a hall pass.

And? A stiff drink for when you're feeling better and have to listen to your kid's Caillou imitations. Poor mama!

makes 1 serving

1½ ounces whiskey

Squeeze of fresh lemon juice

1 teaspoon honey

8 ounces (1 cup) hot tea

Cinnamon stick

Lemon slice, for garnish

Add whiskey, a generous squeeze of lemon, and honey to a mug of tea. Stir until the honey dissolves. Place the cinnamon stick in the mug, and garnish with a lemon slice.

Interrogation Ice

I thought I was kinda smart. I read. I write. I can even do math in my head. But once my son started peppering me with questions like an immigration agent at the border, I realized, oh $hitake mushrooms, I'm sort of a dummy. (Now is not the time to remind me that dummies can raise kids.)

Seriously, I know asking questions is how we learn, but I wasn't prepared for the onslaught. "How big is the ocean?" and "Why don't Max and Ruby have parents?" and "What did the pilgrims use to brush their teeth?" (Oh, oh, I think I know that one! Moonshine? No?)

Listen, little Alex Trebek, this is not what I signed on for. Let's just practice our ABCs and no one gets hurt. (But, a hearty thank-you to my bestie, Google. Without this vehicle making me appear wicked smart to my offspring, where would I be? There is God; then there is Google.)

makes 1 serving

Crushed ice

½ ounce blue curaçao

1 ounce citrus vodka

½ ounce grenadine

Fill a highball glass with crushed ice. Mix the curaçao, vodka, and grenadine and pour over the ice.

Mr. Arse de Leche

Someone help me. Help me find the smug farcehole who coined the phrase "Don't cry over spilled milk." Um, it's my milk and I'll cry if I want to. Glasshalffullkeepingitinperspectivetool?!

I might cry when my toddler knocks an entire gallon of milk off the top shelf of the fridge, which crashes and spills all over the kitchen floor and under the fridge. Have you ever tried to move a fridge while little boys splashed in milk puddles, Mr. Arse de Leche?

I might cry when I leave the kitchen to get my tinkle on and fleetingly think, "Miracles do happen! I'm peeing alone!" when I hear "CRASHBOOM" and find a little scamp fleeing the scene after trying to pour his own milk.

And I'll definitely cry when I've just gotten my kids situated at a restaurant and am actually enjoying the first sip of an adult beverage when BOOM! Milk rains down on half the fam after a spectacular crash.

I don't know who Mr. Arse de Leche is or where he lives. But I do know he does not live with small children. And if I find him, he's getting a gallon to the face, on me! (But don't worry, I won't cry over a little spilled milk …)

makes 1 serving

2 ounces Baileys Irish Cream	*Ice*
1 ounce dark crème de cacao	*5 ounces (⅔ cup) milk*

Stir the Baileys and crème de cacao together in a rocks glass or pint glass with ice, then add the milk.

Butter Boy

I try. I do. I left butter out to soften one day so I could channel my inner June Cleaver and make cookies. I should've known it was way too quiet in the family room—rookie mistake. I peered in and little butter boy had smeared the leather couch (not quite the buttery leather I had in mind) and himself in creamy goodness. Butter boy, 1. Mama, 0.

(Tip: When the house is too quiet, that ain't good.)

There are the stealth attacks, too, like when I had a canister of flour on the counter to make my kids a calzone. (Sidebar: With a toy rolling pin. Because my rolling pin? It was lost in the abyss I call home—probably at the bottom of the black hole of a toy box.) I turn my back to return a phone call (dummy!) and hear a voice chirp, "Uh oh!" and suddenly the canister is upside down in a pile on the floor. I turn my back again (because I am clearly remedial and have yet to learn a thing about toddler terror) to get the vacuum, and he's dancing in the flour and tracking it all over the floor. And laughing. In my face.

I wasn't mad.

makes 1 serving

1 ounce butterscotch schnapps
1 ounce Baileys Irish cream

Pour the schnapps into a shot glass, then carefully pour the Baileys on top. Do not mix. Drink as a shot.

Oedipus Schmedipus

So handsome in his best soccer shirt, he said, "I wanna marry you. I will give you a purse, a caterpillar, and a Mario toy. You're my sweet baboo." Then muah! He smooched me right on the cheek for good measure and stood tall, awaiting my response. His brown eyes sparkled with sincerity. I glanced at the hubs. "I dunno, I'm thinking I should maybe take the deal?"

Hubs laughed, but now my friend calls my four-year-old "Oedipus." Not nice! (His taste in women, though misplaced, is clearly good … ish.)

But crap. Someday a *nonrelative* is going to be dating him for reals. They'll get engaged, she'll find this, and I will soooo look like the batshit crazy mother-in-law.

Hey, HE asked ME!

makes 1 serving

2 ounces vodka	*Ice*
1 ounce Kahlúa	*Half-and-half (to taste)*

Pour the vodka and Kahlúa into a highball glass filled with ice. Add half-and-half to taste.

CHAPTER FIVE

Kindergarten

Shorty is ready for big kid school. Are you? Never mind that you'll probably feel like you ate bad shellfish as the bus pulls away with your baby on it, it's game on for you, too. It's a whole new world to navigate—PTA, fundraising, field trips, sports, and homework. (Dude. I know. Homework in kindergarten.) The transformation from the beginning of the year to the end is crazycakes. And you should see how much progress junior makes, too. Just don't forget to stop and smell the Crayolas, okay? I swear, the older they get, the faster the roller coaster goes.

Orange You Glad You've Got Ice Cubes?

While masquerading as a mad scientist in kindergarten, I saw something on PBS about how to make popsicles with an ice cube tray, orange juice, and toothpicks. Naturally, I filled every single ice cube tray with juice, promptly forgot, and went on to attend to other important business. (*Brady Bunch.* 5 p.m.)

My parents had left me with my older sibs (who very clearly had remedial babysitting skills), and returned home with friends for some after-dinner cocktails to find the only ice available was orange juice ice cubes, and that free babysitting is never really free. Expect the unexpected calamity—and work with it. Behold: Stoli, orange cubes, and Sprite. A star is born! (And a child? Is grounded. No hard feelings, mom.)

makes 1 serving

6 ounces (¾ cup) chilled Sprite (or Diet Sprite if you're watching the muffin top!)

2 ounces orange vodka

Orange juice ice cubes

Orange wheel, for garnish

Pour Sprite and vodka over the orange juice cubes in a highball glass. Garnish with an orange wheel.

Kindergarten Kooler

When my oldest started kindergarten, the bus is what really rattled me. After all my research into the safest car seat, envisioning my "baby" bouncing around unrestrained wasn't easy. I wouldn't drive 100 yards in my car without having him buckled up.

I figured the bus would be what finally broke me. I pictured people blasting around texting/sexting/chomping Whoppers, and not seeing (until it was too late) a bus filled with little kids sans seat belts. When I get nervous about things like this that are out of my control, I rationalize it as a numbers game. How many kids are safely transported every day, in every town, city, and state in America, Canada, Uzbackasomethinstan without incident? Try to remain calm … and enjoy your Kindergarten Kooler.

makes 1 serving

1½ ounces Bacardi rum

6 ounces (¾ cup) chilled fruit punch (or 1 juice box)

2 ounces Pinot Grigio

Ice

Stir the rum, fruit punch, and wine together and serve in a glass over ice.

No Child Left Behind

Do not think the government is not serious about this. Your kindergartner will be hooked on phonics before you finish scarfing that Halloween candy you ~~pilfered~~ borrowed. When I was in kindergarten, we drank chocolate milk and did dot-to-dots. I couldn't even tie my own shoe, never mind read the label on my Toughskins.

At first you'll swell with pride when you're out shopping at Homegoodies and out of nowhere you hear your kindergartner slowly read, "Bed and Bath" on the store wall as you're absentmindedly comparing thread counts. After some high-fiving, you'll sort of forget about how much he's learning, and how quickly. But you'd better think twice about bringing home a tacky joke hat for your BFF from a cheeseball T-shirt shop in Florida, sister. If it says "BEER BITCH" in block letters, you'll find out the hard way that your kid really can read! Then you'll have some 'splaining to do.

makes 1 serving

4 ounces (½ cup) chilled Clamato juice

12 ounces (1½ cups) cold light beer

Pour the Clamato juice into a pint glass. Top with the beer.

Fairy Fo Shizzle Dizzle

The tooth fairy is big biz now. The economy stinks, and the only one giving out cost-of-living increases is, apparently, the tooth fairy. When kindergartner lost his first tooth, hubs decided he'd ask around at work to find out what the going rate for a tooth was. People said anything from $5 to $20. Twenty bucks? I'll yank one of my own teeth out for twenty bucks! (I have a bunch of other ones anyway. I don't need all my teeth to drink my cocktails.)

Also? Don't get busted dropping the dough when little one is snoozing. Remember, they're expecting the tooth fairy and if you're not careful, you can bust up the entire operation. Getting something under the pillow without disturbing the child is harder than it looks, especially if you have a light sleeper. Or a faker! And it's not a night for you to be getting your drink on. Really. One dad I know had too much to drink with his buddies after work and wound up leaving $50 under his kid's pillow by mistake. Served him right!

makes 1 serving

1 ounce Jameson whiskey

1 ounce triple sec

½ ounce sweetened lime juice, such as Rose's

Ice

Lime wheel, for garnish

AFTER you make the tooth/dough exchange, shake the whiskey, triple sec, and sweetened lime juice with ice. Strain and serve in a highball glass over ice. Garnish with a lime wheel.

Sayonara Shandy

I was the youngest in my family. My oldest sister started college when I started kindergarten. (She refused to take me to any cool parties. Rude.) I always envisioned my mom kicking me over the fence into my neighbor's yard to catch the bus and then doing a happy dance, singing, "Free at last!" off-key.

I know that's not true, because I had an ache in the pit of my stomach the day my son left for kindergarten, and I recalled what my mom told me wistfully when he was born: "I swear I blinked and you were in kindergarten." It couldn't be a bigger cliché, but it's true what they say—when you're a mom of young kids, the days are long but the years are short. I didn't realize it until that first day of "real" school arrived.

Your baby is one, then two, then three … "Slooooow down!" you want to scream. It's like a snowball that rolls downhill, picking up momentum and getting bigger as it goes. You hold your breath that when he rolls out of sight, he'll be okay without you, as every bottle, diaper, and sleepless night seems more and more like a distant memory. Bottoms up, mama.

makes 1 serving

6 ounces (¾ cup) chilled lemonade   Ice

6 ounces (¾ cup) cold beer   Lemon wheel, for garnish

Stir together the lemonade and beer and serve over ice in a chilled beer mug. Garnish with a lemon wheel.

2 Sporty 4 Shorty

Do not underestimate the competitive nature of the sports scene for shorties. My friend pointed out that you have parents rolling into the field in cars with license plates like HMERUN, shouting and carrying on, while their kid is picking dandelions in the outfield midgame.

Then you have the parents who are on their crackberries practically the whole time. I can see having to take a call, especially on a work day ... but the whole time? The kids know when you ain't watching—trust me. And so do the coaches, who are giving their time to help your child.

Most coaches are great, but there are a few who want to win at any cost. I may have the coordination of a wild buffalo, but when kids are little, I think all that should matter is that they have fun. My friend who coaches soccer received an e-mail after a game accusing him of running up the score when his team beat the other by four goals. Lighten up, Francis! Your kid is not going pro. Let him have fun, and show you care by watching. And for cripes sake, go home and have a cocktail! It's not that complicated.

makes 1 serving

2 ounces vodka

6 ounces (¾ cup) chilled Gatorade (pick your color)

Ice

Stir together the vodka and Gatorade in a highball glass filled with ice.

PTA Mama Jama

On weekend mornings in college, one of our friends—we'll call him Pat—would call everyone's apartment (how '90s) to find out who saw who with whom, doing what, where, and why the night before. He got the deets like a stalkerazzi in training at TMZ. (Sweet Jesus in heaven above, thank you that smartphones were not even a thought in the '90s!) We dubbed Pat "PTA mom."

If you volunteer at your child's school because you sincerely want to help, rock on. There are plenty of opportunities. The point is to help the teachers and, by extension, the kids. You SO don't want to be the mom standing on the sidelines scoping out everyone's shoes, blabbing about your ten-day Caribbean cruise, and outing the mom who threw too many back at Bunco. In short, don't be a Pat! The glory days? Are over, sunshine. It ain't about you anymore.

makes 12 servings

2 cups strong black tea

1½ cups sugar

6 ounces frozen orange juice concentrate

12 ounces frozen lemonade concentrate

2 cups water

2 to 3 cups bourbon (to your taste)

Chilled Sprite

In a sealable freezer container, stir together all but the Sprite and freeze for at least 6 hours. Take out of the freezer, blend to soften, and scoop into a glass. Add Sprite to produce the desired consistency and taste. Makes plenty for all your new PTA pals!

School Supply Slammer

You'll probably receive a list of supplies to buy junior before school starts. Before I had kids, I assumed our taxes paid for that stuff. Who knew? I guess communities have more pressing issues to attend to than educating our youth or, as I like to refer to those pesky kids, the future of our country.

So the list! It was extensive and chock-full of stuff I never heard of—I was zigging and zagging looking for things like 2-gallon Ziplocs, fancy pencils, and odd-shaped boxes. Holy muffin tops! I looked like I ran a 5K (I mean, if I ever were to run a 5K. *Cough*) by the time I finished, crumpled list in hand. Vindication came when my smartypants friends slowly started to grouse that they had to make trips to multiple stores and still couldn't find everything. I decided school supply shopping is like a bad scavenger hunt without the booze. I say we make it a party next time. (I'll bring the Slammers if you hunt down the Ziplocs.)

makes 1 serving

1 ounce Southern Comfort   *Ice*

1 ounce sloe gin   *Orange twist, for garnish*

2 ounces orange juice

Shake the Southern Comfort, sloe gin, and orange juice with ice. Strain into a highball glass with ice. Garnish with an orange twist.

Fundraiser Flop

Know that you will be forced to sell some cheaptastic fundraising crap on behalf of your kid for a 278 percent markup. When I was a wee chump, my parents refused to hawk my wares for me—I got my door-to-door salesgirl on. (The Jehovah's Witnesses would've been proud. I totally brought it. I left no doorbell unrung.) But now, sending kindergartners out into sketchy suburban cul-de-sacs where Toyota minivans roll blaring Michael Bublé is frowned upon. In fact, the materials they send home specifically say something like, "Please don't go door to door. Safety first! Meep!" in case reckless parents today even contemplate making their kids go all old skool and tear up the pavement.

And you have to know it's bad form to sell to the sellers, aka your neighbors with kids in the same school/activities. So get your checkbook and your cocktail ready—you'll be doing some shopping. Buy your processed frankencheese product, see-through wrapping paper, and subscription to the most interesting obscure magazine you never heard of without ever leaving the comfort of your home. Now don't be a cheapo—it's for the children!

makes 1 serving

½ (12-ounce) bottle cold lager beer

½ (12-ounce) bottle chilled cider, dry or sweet

Stir the beer and cider together in a pint glass and enjoy.

Field Trip Fiesta

Let's talk about field trips. You know you're just dying to get back on one of those big yellow buses. And here's a fun fact: Nothing makes you realize childbirth has taken its toll like a bumpy bus ride after a 16-ounce coffee. I hope you listened to your OB and did your Kegels, girl! (I know, right? I don't have time to exercise the parts of my body that show, never mind my private bits!)

If your bladder survives the ride, your head might not. Three dozen screeching kids and a few cackling mamas … ouchie. So pack some aspirin with your Depends. You'll be a hero on the ride home. (Bonus points for a flask. Just kidding!)

If you survive the bus ride intact, you realize how much responsibility you have. You don't want to overstep your bounds with other people's kids. Yelling things like, "Hey motormouthantsinhispants (oh crap, that was my kid), sit yo ass down and listen!" is definitely frowned upon. But hey, if you keep everyone safe and remember to have fun, so what if you peep your pants a little?

makes 1 serving

1 ounce light rum

2 ounces chilled pineapple juice

1 ounce blue curaçao

1 ounce cream of coconut

1 cup ice

Pineapple slice, for garnish

Maraschino cherry, for garnish

Blend together the rum, pineapple juice, curaçao, cream of coconut, and ice in a blender. Serve in a tall glass, garnished with a pineapple slice and/or cherry.

Nerf Swizzle

Dry your tears! Celebrate the day! Your little scholar is on his way! Ok, ok. That's momspeak for: everyone has back-to-school shindigs now. Once you get over the bus anxiety and come to grips with the realization that your baby ain't a baby anymore (hold me!), you'll probably feel the way most moms do: happy to be back in a routine. And despite their back-to-school jitters, even the kids are glad to be back with their buddies.

At my friend's party, the moms chatted about ~~Coach Taylor from *Friday Night Lights*~~ European economic challenges while the kids played on the Slip 'n Slide and unloaded about 1000 Nerf bullets into her yard. My neighbor had so much fun that she didn't realize until she walked all the way home that she had a Nerf bullet in her hair. Hopefully the PTA Mama Jama didn't see her!

makes 4 servings

8 ounces Gosling's Black Seal rum

6 dashes angostura bitters

Juice of 2 lemons

5 ounces (⅔ cup) chilled pineapple juice

5 ounces (⅔ cup) chilled orange juice

2 ounces grenadine

Ice

Maraschino cherries, for garnish

Shake together the rum, bitters, juices, and grenadine until the head is frothing. Strain into glasses filled with ice. Garnish each with a cherry. Makes enough for all the mamas.

STFU Slushie

When you have more than one child of the same sex, or multiples, it's an invitation for random acquaintances to share their thoughts. Some of the many comments my friends with multiples have encountered:

"Are those natural, or did you do fertility treatments?"

"I hope your husband makes A LOT of money!"

O to the M to the G.

Having three boys seems to elicit tons of comments, too. Most are kind, but some are just plain rude. And are said … in front of my boys. Who might try my patience at times, but they're sweet and loving, and most of all, people, *they all can totally hear what you're saying!*

My personal fave was from a waitress after dinner, where, I swear on all things holy, the boys were SO good.

"Three boys!" she bellowed, shaking her head back and forth and staring at them as though they were a science experiment gone awry. "Did you mean to do that?"

Um? I did mean to do that. Yes, yes, I did. I did it three times, baby. And each time I ordered a boy.

"Hi God?"

"Yes, my child."

"What up? Tell my peeps I said hi, I love them, and I miss them. But let me cut to the chase because you're a busy guy. I need to order another boy. Stat."

"You got it, girl!"

"Thanks, God. You're the best!"

makes 16 servings

4 cups water

12 ounces frozen lemonade concentrate

6 ounces frozen cranberry juice concentrate

1 cup sugar

1 (750 ml) bottle vodka

At least 8 hours before serving, in a sealable freezer container, stir together all ingredients. Freeze. When ready to serve, remove from the freezer and blend to the desired consistency. Makes enough to share with the choir of angels.

Conclusion

Being a mom is, and always will be, my proudest accomplishment. It's not a glamorous gig, the pay stinks, and sometimes the subordinates … are less than gracious. Sometimes I feel like I have it all figured out, only to wake up the next day feeling like an abysmal failure. I know I'm not running a corporation. I don't have shareholders to answer to. But somewhere between wiping noses and tushes, I realized I'm putting people out into the world. And damn, I just want them to be my best work. The foundation starts here—who knows how high and how far they can go?

You know, being a mom isn't for the faint of heart. You need to be willing to be a human Kleenex, sit up all night rocking a sick baby, and chase younger kids around the perimeter of a Little League field while an older one plays—and you'd best be watching that older one play, because he'll be asking on the car ride home if you saw him hit that ball. You need to be prepared to miss adult parties at the last minute because … wait for it … someone puked in your hand after you got all glammed up and had visions of adult conversations dancing in your head. You'll need to stay home and read *Wacky Wednesday* 217 times instead. You might figure out that you'll have to work two jobs someday to put them through college. And you might be lucky if that's the hardest thing you'll have to do.

But the weird thing is, you won't care (most of the time!) that you caught puke in your hand, missed a fantastic party, or chased a baby around a Little League field. All it takes is one little face to beam at you and say, "I love you, Mommy!" to make it worthwhile. They'll know you were there, doing things right and, yeah, making mistakes as you muddled through. Trying and loving and hoping and wishing.

What stretch marks?!

Whatever your personal story is as a mom, I know you'll have *those days*. Those moments. Those calamities. You might wonder, "Oh my God, what have I done?!" You'll laugh. You'll cry. You'll beam. You might fantasize fleetingly about running away from home.

There will be times when you need a break. When you just can't sing the *Caillou* theme song one more time, lest you wind up in a straitjacket. When the whining has reached a peak. And the walls feel like they're closing in. You're a mom—not a martyr. Needing a break from your kids doesn't make you a bad mom. Moms take care of everyone. Sometimes we need to take a break to take care of ourselves, even if it's just putting our feet up with a cocktail and a good book. Sometimes we need a moms' night out or even a moms' night in with friends who we know we can vent to and laugh with—who we know will get it. Most of us aren't airbrushed celebs with personal chefs and personal trainers. We can't blast out feeling like a million bucks in designer jeans that cost as much as our weekly groceries.

This book is for you—for all of the regular moms out there, slugging it out every day, hoping and wishing they're getting it right. I hope you put your feet up and have a yummy drink and a laugh, mama. You deserve it!

Conversions

MEASURE	EQUIVALENT	METRIC
1 teaspoon	--	5 milliliters
1 tablespoon	3 teaspoons	14.8 milliliters
1 cup	16 tablespoons	236.8 milliliters
1 pint	2 cups	473.6 milliliters
1 quart	4 cups	947.2 milliliters
1 liter	4 cups + 3½ tablespoons	1000 milliliters
1 ounce (liquid)	⅛ cup	29.57 milliliters
1 pound	16 ounces	453.49 grams

Photo Credits

All photos listed below are from shutterstock.com.

page 11: © dean bertoncelj

page 12: © wacpan

page 13: © John Clark

page 21: © Michael C. Gray

page 22: © Momentum

page 27: © Elena Itsenko

page 29: © margouillat photo

page 34: baby pictures in photograph
   © John Wollwerth

page 42: © Stanislav V.

page 45: © Sally Scott

page 68: © Elena Schweitzer

page 84: © Anton Prado PHOTO

page 90: © Nancy Hixson

page 109: © Elena Elisseeva

page 110: © photopixel

Acknowledgments

Thank you to Holly Schmidt and Allan Penn for plucking me out of the blogosphere and recognizing I had the right voice for this project. To the folks at Ulysses Press: The book looks better than I ever could have imagined. Also? I'm thirsty now.

Thank you to my parents, Colette and the late Ed Twohig, for giving me the best gift you can give anyone: a sense of humor. Many thanks to Lisa Wallace, Monique Ackley, and Dave Visnick for creating a kick-butt blog for me. To Lauren Minichino, Sue Heimberg, Rita Malloy, and Dawn Weber for providing feedback on the book while in progress—a sincere thanks. To Amelia Sauter, my favorite bartender/writer, for the invaluable expertise. Meegs Pagliarulo, Rebecca Chase, Colette Arnold, Clare Duross, Michelle Kaelin, and Kim Pleticha for your support. Kathy Fontanella, Molly Brennan, Ange Moya, and Kate Bouchard, for never even flinching when I said I'd write a book someday—thanks! To my readers at www.muffintopmommy.com—you rock!

To Rick, my hubs/baby daddy/BF/drinking buddy, I wouldn't want to be on this parenting adventure with anyone but you. To my three boys, thank you for making me laugh every day. No amount of household damage or muddy cleats can make me forget: I am blessed and I love you.

About the Author

JANET FRONGILLO lives in New Hampshire with her husband, three sons, and assorted dust bunnies. She is a regular humor writer for *Parent: Wise Austin*. When she's not blowing the budget at Target or dreaming up cocktails on the sidelines at tee ball practice, she can be found blogging at www.muffintopmommy.com.